PORTUGAL

TRAVEL GUIDE

2023

A Comprehensive, Practical Guide to Planning Your Dream Vacation in Portugal for the year 2023

SARAFINA PAWLAK

PORTUGAL TRAVEL GUIDE 2023

INTRODUCTION

CHAPTER ONE

- DISCOVER THE CHARMS OF PORTUGAL: AN INTRODUCTION TO THE LAND OF ENCHANTMENT!

- EXPLORE THE DIVERSE POPULATION AND VIBRANT CULTURE OF PORTUGAL!

- UNLOCK THE SECRETS OF YOUR NEXT EXCITING ADVENTURE BY PLANNING YOUR JOURNEY

- UNLOCK THE MAGIC OF PORTUGAL - CHOOSE YOUR ADVENTURE!

CHAPTER 2

SARAFINA PAWLAK

PORTUGAL TRAVEL GUIDE 2023

SARAFINA PAWLAK

PORTUGAL TRAVEL GUIDE 2023

SARAFINA PAWLAK

PORTUGAL TRAVEL GUIDE 2023

- ## CHAPTER 9

CONCLUSION

SARAFINA PAWLAK

PORTUGAL TRAVEL GUIDE 2023

INTRODUCTION

It was a sunny morning in Portugal when I first stepped foot on the cobblestone streets. I had been planning this trip for months and finally, here I was experiencing the culture and beauty of a place I'd only dreamed of visiting.

As I made my way through the winding streets, I couldn't help but be in awe of the architecture and the beauty of the city. Everywhere I looked there seemed to be something new and exciting to explore. From the brightly colored buildings to the intricate tile work, it was all so captivating.

I made my way to the waterfront where I could see the waves crashing against the shore. The sound of the ocean was so soothing and calming. I was in awe of the beauty of this place. I felt a sense of peace, something I had been searching for in my life.

That day, I decided to take a boat tour around the coastline. As we sailed, I watched as the sun set in the distance. The sky was ablaze with an array of colors and it was one of the most beautiful sights I had ever seen.

As the night drew near, I decided to explore the city's nightlife. I found myself in the midst of a lively street filled with music and laughter. Everywhere I looked there were

SARAFINA PAWLAK

locals enjoying the night out with friends and family.

The following days were spent exploring the city and its culture. I made sure to take in the sights and sounds of this beautiful country. From the cuisine to the people, I was mesmerized by the way of life here in Portugal.

The time I spent in Portugal changed me in ways I could never have imagined. I felt a sense of belonging and peace. I had found a place I could call home. I was able to look at life in a whole new light and was able to appreciate the beauty of the world around me.

I left Portugal with a newfound appreciation for life. I had experienced a culture I had only dreamed of and it changed my life in ways I couldn't have imagined. This trip was one of the most valuable experiences of my life and I will forever cherish the memories I made during my time in Portugal.

SARAFINA PAWLAK

PORTUGAL TRAVEL GUIDE 2023

CHAPTER ONE

DISCOVER THE CHARMS OF PORTUGAL: AN INTRODUCTION TO THE LAND OF ENCHANTMENT!

Portugal is an incredibly beautiful country located on the Iberian Peninsula in southwestern Europe. It is bordered by the Atlantic Ocean to the west and south and by Spain to the east and north. Portugal has a long and fascinating history, with its first documented inhabitants being the Celts in the 4th century BC. Throughout its history, Portugal has been a major trading and cultural hub and has been home to many different cultures and religions.

Portugal is known for its stunning beaches, mountainous landscapes, vibrant cities, and captivating culture.

The country has everything from stunning beaches in the Algarve region, to the culturally rich capital city of Lisbon, to the stunning mountain villages of the Serra de Estrela mountain range. Portugal is also known for its excellent cuisine, including fresh seafood, hearty stews, and delicious pastries.

Portugal is an excellent destination for tourists seeking an authentic experience. The country has a wealth of cultural attractions, including world-class museums, historic castles, and ancient churches.

SARAFINA PAWLAK

PORTUGAL TRAVEL GUIDE 2023

Visitors can explore the cobblestone streets of Lisbon, visit the picturesque villages of the Azores Islands, and experience the unique culture of the Algarve.

Portugal has a temperate climate with mild winters and hot summers. The country has an extensive public transportation system, including buses, trains, and ferries. The capital, Lisbon, is a major transport hub, and other cities in Portugal are connected to the rest of Europe through an extensive rail network.

Whether you're looking for an exciting nightlife scene, an authentic cultural experience, or a relaxing beach holiday,

Portugal has something for everyone. From its stunning landscapes to its vibrant cities, Portugal is a country full of charm, beauty, and adventure.

GEOGRAPHY AND CLIMATE

Geography and climate play an important role in planning a successful vacation. When deciding where to vacation, it's important to consider the geographical features of the area, such as the terrain, its proximity to the ocean, and its climate.

When it comes to terrain, the landscape of an area can be a major factor when deciding where to go. Different areas have different features that make them unique.

SARAFINA PAWLAK

PORTUGAL TRAVEL GUIDE
2023

For example, mountain ranges, deserts, and glaciers can all be found in certain parts of the world. Depending on what type of activity you're interested in, different terrain types may be more or less ideal.

The proximity to the ocean is also an important factor. Areas close to the ocean typically have milder climates than those inland and can offer the perfect combination of sun and sea. Coastal areas are often great for activities like swimming, surfing, and fishing.

The climate of an area is a major factor and can determine the type of vacation you'll have. Areas with temperate climates are ideal for outdoor activities like hiking, biking, and camping. Warmer climates are great for beach trips and water sports.

Colder climates are good for winter sports and activities like skiing and snowboarding.

When planning a vacation, it's important to keep geography and climate in mind. Doing your research and understanding the features of an area can help you make the best decision for your vacation. With a little planning and knowledge, you can create the perfect vacation experience.

EXPLORE THE DIVERSE POPULATION AND VIBRANT CULTURE OF PORTUGAL!

Portugal is a country with a rich and diverse culture and population. Located on the Iberian Peninsula, Portugal is bordered by

SARAFINA PAWLAK

PORTUGAL TRAVEL GUIDE
2023

Spain and the Atlantic Ocean. With a population of over 10 million, it is the world's 11th most populous country.

The population of Portugal is composed of many ethnicities, including Portuguese, Sephardic Jews, African, and Brazilian. Portuguese is the official language, though many other languages are also spoken. The majority of the population is Roman Catholic, but there are also smaller numbers of other Christian denominations, Muslims, Hindus, and Buddhists.

Portuguese culture is an eclectic mix of many different influences. There are strong cultural ties to Spain, as well as to the former colonies in Africa and South America. The culture has also been heavily influenced by the country's maritime history, as well as its traditional fishing industry.

The people of Portugal are known for their hospitality and friendliness, and their cuisine is highly regarded. Traditional dishes include bacalhau (salted cod fish), caldo verde (a soup made with kale, potatoes, and chorizo), and port wine.

Portugal is also home to many festivals, such as the National Festivals of Music and Dance in Lisbon, the Festival of Popular Music in Braga, and the Carnival of Lisbon. The country also has a thriving arts scene, with a number of museums, galleries, and theaters.

SARAFINA PAWLAK

PORTUGAL TRAVEL GUIDE 2023

Portugal is a fascinating destination for travelers interested in exploring the culture and population of this unique country. From its vibrant cities to its small towns and villages, Portugal offers a wealth of cultural experiences. Whether you're looking for historical sites, traditional cuisine, or just a relaxing holiday in the sun, you'll find plenty to explore in Portugal.

UNLOCK THE SECRETS OF YOUR NEXT EXCITING ADVENTURE BY PLANNING YOUR JOURNEY

If you're planning a trip to Portugal, you'll want to make sure you make the most of your time in this beautiful country. Portugal is home to stunning landscapes, unique cuisine, and a vibrant culture, and with the right planning, you can make sure to experience all that Portugal has to offer. Here's what you need to know to plan the perfect trip to Portugal.

UNLOCK THE MAGIC OF PORTUGAL - CHOOSE YOUR ADVENTURE!

The first step in planning your trip to Portugal is to decide where you want to go. Portugal is a large country, with a variety of different regions and cities to explore. If you're looking for a beach vacation, head to the Algarve region, where you can soak up the sun on some of the country's most stunning beaches. If you're more interested in exploring cities, Lisbon and Porto are

PORTUGAL TRAVEL GUIDE 2023

both great choices, with plenty of history, culture, and nightlife.

CHAPTER 2

EXPERIENCE PORTUGAL'S WONDERS - BOOK YOUR ACCOMMODATION NOW!

Once you've chosen your destination, it's time to book your accommodation. Portugal is home to dozens of hotels, guesthouses, and hostels, so you'll have no trouble finding the perfect place to stay. Be sure to read reviews and compare prices to make sure you get the best deal,

EMBARK ON AN EXCITING JOURNEY TO PORTUGAL: PLAN YOUR TRANSPORTATION NOW

SARAFINA PAWLAK

PORTUGAL TRAVEL GUIDE 2023

Once you've booked your accommodation, it's time to plan your transportation. Portugal has an extensive public transportation system, with buses, trains, and trams all available to get you around the country. If you're traveling between cities, you can also take advantage of Portugal's many low-cost airlines, such as Ryanair, EasyJet, and TAP Portugal.

MAKE AN ITINERARY

Once you have your transportation sorted, it's time to make your itinerary. Portugal is home to many different attractions, from ancient cities to stunning beaches, so you'll want to make sure you have enough time to experience everything you want to. Make a list of all the places you want to visit, and then plan out your days so you don't miss anything.

PACK APPROPRIATELY

Finally, it's time to pack your bags. Portugal is a warm country, so be sure to pack plenty of lightweight, breathable clothing. You should also bring a light jacket and umbrella, just in case it rains. Be sure to also pack sunscreen, insect repellent, and any other necessary items.

By following these tips, you'll be well on your way to planning the perfect trip to Portugal. From choosing your destination to packing your bags, you'll be able to make the most of your time in this beautiful country. So get ready to explore Portugal and all it has to offer!

SARAFINA PAWLAK

PORTUGAL TRAVEL GUIDE 2023

CHAPTER 3

DISCOVERING THE UNIQUE CULTURAL IDENTITY OF PORTUGAL: LANGUAGE AND RELIGION

Portugal is a country renowned for its diverse and vibrant culture, and this is reflected in the many languages and religions which can be experienced within its borders.

The official language of Portugal is Portuguese, a Romance language derived from Latin. Portuguese is spoken by almost all of the population and is used in all public and official contexts. It is a language of great beauty and elegance and is used in literature, music and the arts.

In addition to Portuguese, there are also several other languages spoken in Portugal, particularly in the north and south regions of the country. Galician is spoken in the north by around four million people, and is derived from the same Latin root as Portuguese. In the south, the dialects of Alentejo and Algarve are still spoken, although their use is slowly decreasing.

Religion has also played an important role in the history and culture of Portugal. The majority of the population is Roman Catholic, and the Portuguese are very proud of their religious heritage. The country is also home to a number of other religious minorities, including Protestantism, Judaism and Islam.

SARAFINA PAWLAK

PORTUGAL TRAVEL GUIDE 2023

The diversity of languages and religions in Portugal make it a fascinating destination for travelers. Whether you wish to explore the beautiful Portuguese language, learn about the country's religious history, or experience its vibrant culture, Portugal has something to offer to everyone.

DISCOVER THE ENCHANTING DESTINATIONS OF PORTUGAL!

Portugal is a small country located in the southwestern corner of Europe, but it packs a big punch when it comes to breathtaking sights, delicious cuisine and vibrant culture. From rugged coastlines and sweeping beaches to historic cities and charming rural towns, there's something for everyone in Portugal. Whether you're looking for a relaxing beach getaway or an adventure-filled cultural journey, Portugal has something to offer. Here are some of the top destinations in Portugal to consider for your next vacation.

SARAFINA PAWLAK

PORTUGAL TRAVEL GUIDE 2023

LISBON

The bustling capital of Portugal, Lisbon is the perfect destination for culture lovers. With a history stretching back over two millennia, the city is home to a wealth of historical sites, stunning architecture and vibrant nightlife. From the iconic yellow trams winding their way through the narrow streets to the breathtaking views of the Tagus River, visitors will find plenty of things to do in Lisbon. Don't miss out on the city's excellent restaurants, cafes and bars, which serve up some of the best seafood in the world.

PORTO

Porto is Portugal's second largest city and the birthplace of port wine. Located on the Douro River, the city is known for its vibrant nightlife, cobblestone streets and iconic wine cellars. Visitors should also take the time to explore the Ribeira district, which is home to some of the city's most beautiful churches and bridges. Don't forget to take a day trip to the nearby city of Guimaraes, which is known as the birthplace of Portugal.

THE ALGARVE

The Algarve is Portugal's most popular beach destination. Stretching along the southern coast of the country, it's home to some of Europe's most stunning beaches. From the dramatic cliffs of Cabo de Sao Vicente to the secluded coves of Alvor, there's something for everyone in the Algarve. The region is also home to some excellent golf courses, as well as a vibrant nightlife scene.

SARAFINA PAWLAK

PORTUGAL TRAVEL GUIDE 2023

MADEIRA

Madeira is an autonomous region of Portugal located off the coast of Morocco. The island is known for its lush, green landscapes, stunning beaches and warm climate. Visitors should take the time to explore the island's winding roads and quaint villages, as well as the many excellent restaurants. Don't forget to take a cable car ride to the top of Pico Ruivo, which offers spectacular views of the entire island.

THE AZORES

The Azores are a chain of islands located in the middle of the Atlantic Ocean. While the islands are relatively unknown to most travelers, they're home to some of the most beautiful and unspoiled landscapes in Europe. From lush forests and volcanic peaks to crystal-clear lakes and thermal hot springs, the Azores offer something for everyone. Whether you're looking for a relaxing beach getaway or an adventure-filled hiking trip, the Azores have something to offer.

No matter where you choose to go in Portugal, you're sure to find plenty of things to do. Whether you're looking for a relaxing beach vacation or a cultural journey through the country's fascinating history and culture, Portugal is sure to have something for everyone.

SARAFINA PAWLAK

CHAPTER 4

THE LIVELY BEATS AND VIBRANT MOVES OF PORTUGAL'S MUSICAL AND DANCE CULTURE

Music and dance are two of the most important elements of Portuguese culture. From traditional folk songs to contemporary pop and hip-hop, Portugal's music scene is incredibly diverse and dynamic. Music is a source of pride and identity for Portugal, with a rich and varied history of songs and styles.

Traditional Portuguese folk music is a vibrant and lively form of music, characterized by a strong influence from

African and Latin American rhythms. Fado, a traditional style of music indigenous to Portugal, is a popular genre that has been around for centuries. It is usually performed by a singer accompanied by a single guitar and is characterized by darkly romantic lyrics and a slow, melancholic rhythm.

In the past few decades, Portugal has become a major player in the world of popular music. Portuguese pop and hip-hop are popular throughout the country, with a number of young and talented artists making waves in the music industry. Portugal has also become a major destination for international dance music, with a thriving club and festival scene.

SARAFINA PAWLAK

PORTUGAL TRAVEL GUIDE 2023

Dance is an integral part of Portuguese culture, with numerous traditional styles and dances originating from different regions of the country. Some of the most popular forms of traditional dance in Portugal are Fandango, a flamenco-style dance from the North of Portugal, and the Chula, a lively and contagious dance from the Algarve region.

Portugal is home to many popular music and dance festivals throughout the year, and visitors are sure to find a wide range of events to choose from. From traditional folk music festivals to modern club and electronic music events, there is something for everyone. Portugal is also the perfect place to learn and experience traditional Portuguese music and dance, with many classes and workshops available all over the country.

No matter what type of music or dance you are interested in, Portugal is sure to have something to offer. From traditional folk music to modern electronic music, visitors to Portugal can experience the country's rich musical heritage and vibrant dance culture.

SARAFINA PAWLAK

PORTUGAL TRAVEL GUIDE 2023

EXPLORING PORTUGUESE NATURE

Portugal is country rich in natural beauty, with a variety of landscapes and wildlife that make it an ideal destination for nature lovers. The country has something for everyone. Whether you are looking for a relaxed beach vacation or an adventure into the wild, Portugal has it all.

The coastline of Portugal is particularly interesting, with a variety of beaches, cliffs, and coves to explore. The beaches are among the best in Europe, and are perfect for swimming, surfing, fishing, and even sailing. The cliffs offer breathtaking views, and many of them are great for rock climbing. The coves are hidden gems, providing a peaceful oasis away from the hustle and bustle of the cities.

The inland areas of Portugal are equally as beautiful, with lush forests and rolling hills. These areas are great for hiking, biking, and camping. The trails are well maintained and the scenery is breathtaking. There are also a number of national parks and nature reserves, which are perfect for wildlife viewing. Many of these areas are home to a variety of birds and other animals, including wolves, lynxes, and otters.

In the northern parts of Portugal, the mountains are a highlight. The Serra da Estrela is the highest mountain range in Portugal, and the views from the summit are spectacular. The range is home to a variety of wildlife, and it is a popular destination for mountain climbers. The Peneda-Geres National Park is also located in the northern parts of the country, and it is a great place to explore the wild side of Portugal.

For those looking for a more relaxed experience, Portugal is home to a variety of wine regions, which are perfect for wine tasting and exploring. The Douro Valley is one of the most famous, and is known for its red and white wines. The Alentejo region is another popular wine region, and it is home to some of the best wines in the country.

No matter what type of nature experience you are looking for, Portugal has something for everyone. Whether you are looking for a relaxing beach vacation or an adventure into the wild, Portugal has it all. So don't wait any longer – start exploring the natural beauty of Portugal today

SARAFINA PAWLAK

PORTUGAL TRAVEL GUIDE 2023

BEACHES

Portugal is well-known for having some of the best beaches in the world. With its miles of pristine coastlines, Portugal is a paradise for beach-lovers. From the golden sandy beaches of the Algarve to the wild and rugged coasts of the north, you'll discover a wealth of stunning beach spots.

In the south, the Algarve region is a well-known holiday destination and home to some of the most beautiful beaches in Portugal. Golden sands, crystal-clear waters and plenty of activities make it the perfect spot for a relaxing beach holiday. The Algarve is home to some of the most popular beach spots in Portugal, including

Praia da Rocha, Praia da Marinha and Praia da Falesia.

Heading north, the beaches in Portugal become more rugged. The north is home to some of the most dramatic and wild beaches in the country. From the long golden sands of Praia do Areal in the Minho region to the wild and remote beaches of the Azores and Madeira, you'll find plenty of stunning spots to explore.

Portugal also has plenty of secluded and remote beaches, perfect for those looking for a more peaceful beach experience. The western coast of the country is home to several stunning, untouched beaches, including Praia de Alvor and Praia do Amado in the Algarve region.

SARAFINA PAWLAK

PORTUGAL TRAVEL GUIDE
2023

No matter where you go in Portugal, you're sure to find a beach that fits your needs. With its miles of coastline, Portugal is a beach-lovers paradise. Whether you're looking for a beach that is perfect for relaxing or one that is full of adventure, Portugal has it all. So grab your towel and your sunscreen and get ready to explore the stunning beaches of Portugal.

FLORA AND FAUNA.

Portugal is a beautiful country with a unique and diverse range of flora and fauna. From its expansive coastal regions to its lush mountain ranges, Portugal has something to offer to nature lovers of all kinds.

For those interested in plants, Portugal's flora is incredibly diverse. The country has a wide array of native plant species, ranging from the vibrant wildflowers of the Serra de Estrela to the subtropical palm trees of the Algarve. Portugal also has many exotic species, such as the giant cacti of Madeira and the lush bamboo forests of the Azores.

SARAFINA PAWLAK

PORTUGAL TRAVEL GUIDE 2023

For wildlife enthusiasts, Portugal offers a rich variety of fauna. The country's coastal waters are home to a number of marine mammals, including dolphins, whales, and seals. Land-based animals such as wild boar, Iberian lynx, and red deer can be found in many of Portugal's national parks and nature reserves. Bird-watchers will also find plenty to see, with over 500 species of birds recorded in the country.

Whether you're a plant enthusiast or an animal lover, Portugal has something to offer. From its unique flora and fauna to its stunning landscapes, Portugal is a paradise for nature lovers.

MOUNTAINS.

Portugal is a breathtaking country with a variety of landscapes, from beaches to mountains, which make it a great destination for adventurers. Within its boundaries, there are dozens of mountains and mountain ranges, many of which offer amazing opportunities for hiking and other outdoor activities.

The Serra da Estrela, or 'Star Mountain Range', is the highest mountain range in Portugal and mainland Portugal. It is located in the central-northeastern part of the country, and is home to the highest peak in the mainland, the Torre. It is a

SARAFINA PAWLAK

popular destination for hiking, with its peaks offering amazing views of the surrounding countryside. It is also a great spot for skiing and snowboarding in the winter months.

The Serra da Lousa is located in the northeast of Portugal, and is a popular destination for rock climbing and abseiling. It is also home to some of the most stunning natural scenery in the country, with its lush forests and rugged mountain peaks. It is a great spot for those looking for an adventure, as it offers a variety of activities from climbing to camping.

The mountains of the Azores are located in the middle of the Atlantic Ocean, and are known for their spectacular scenery and unique wildlife. The highest peak in the Azores is the Pico Mountain, which stands at almost 2400 meters. It is a popular destination for hikers, as its slopes offer stunning views of the surrounding ocean.

The Serra de Sintra is located in the western part of Portugal, and is home to some of the most beautiful mountains in the country. It is a great destination for hikers, with its lush forests and stunning views of the surrounding countryside. It is also home to some of Portugal's most well-known castles, such as the Pena Palace and the Moorish Castle of the Sintra Mountains.

These are just some of the many mountains in Portugal, each offering something unique and special. Whether you're looking for an

SARAFINA PAWLAK

PORTUGAL TRAVEL GUIDE 2023

adventure or just want to take in the stunning scenery, Portugal's mountains offer something for everyone. So make sure to explore them on your next visit to Portugal!

SARAFINA PAWLAK

PORTUGAL TRAVEL GUIDE 2023

CHAPTER 5

THE JOYOUS EXPERIENCE OF SHOPPING AND ENTERTAINMENT IN PORTUGAL!

Shopping and entertainment in Portugal are among the most varied and exciting of any European destination. Portugal is a country of diverse culture, cuisine, and entertainment, making it an ideal place for visitors to explore. From large shopping malls to smaller boutiques and flea markets, Portugal offers something for everyone.

When it comes to shopping, Portugal is home to a wealth of unique stores. From high-end fashion boutiques to vintage shops, Portugal has something for every style and budget. Lisbon, the capital city of

Portugal, is home to a wide variety of shopping malls and stores, including the Armazéns do Chiado, one of the oldest shopping malls in the city. For more traditional shopping, visitors can explore the winding streets of Alfama, the old historic district of Lisbon, and visit the city's many charming markets.

For entertainment, Portugal offers a wide range of activities and attractions. Visitors can explore the country's stunning coastline and golden beaches, or experience the vibrant nightlife of Lisbon and Porto. Portugal is also home to a variety of cultural attractions, from world-famous museums to scenic parks. Visitors can also enjoy the country's renowned food and wine scene, with a variety of restaurants, bars, and wineries to explore.

SARAFINA PAWLAK

PORTUGAL TRAVEL GUIDE 2023

Portugal is a great destination for both shopping and entertainment. With its varied culture and attractions, Portugal is the perfect place for visitors to explore and experience something new. Whether you're looking for unique boutiques, vibrant nightlife, or stunning natural scenery, Portugal has something for everyone.

CUSINES

Portugal is a country full of diverse culinary traditions, from the rustic regional dishes of the countryside to the seafood-laden Mediterranean-style cuisine of the coastal regions. The country's cuisine has been shaped by its location, with influences from its former colonies, and its proximity to the Atlantic Ocean. In Portugal, traditional dishes are often simple, but packed with flavor.

The cornerstone of Portuguese cooking is the use of fresh, local ingredients. Freshly caught seafood, such as cod, sardines, and tuna, are staples of the coastal cuisine. Fresh vegetables, such as tomatoes, potatoes, and onions, are often used to create hearty stews and soups. Chickpeas, lentils, and other legumes are also popular ingredients. Portuguese cooking often involves a healthy dose of garlic, paprika, and olive oil.

Popular dishes include bacalhau (salted cod), caldo verde (a green soup made of potatoes and kale), feijoada (a stew of beans, pork, and sausage), and cozido à portuguesa (a pork and vegetable stew). Portuguese cuisine is also known for its desserts, such as pastéis de nata (custard tarts), bolo de arroz (rice cake), and the famous Portuguese egg tarts.

Wine is an essential part of Portuguese cuisine. The country is home to hundreds of wineries, producing some of the world's most renowned wines, such as Douro, Vinho Verde, and Dão. Other popular beverages include ginjinha (sour cherry liqueur) and port (fortified wine).

Portugal is also home to some of the world's best restaurants. From Michelin-starred establishments to traditional taverns, the country has something to offer every type of traveler. The Algarve region is particularly renowned for its seafood dishes, while Lisbon is known for its hip and trendy eateries.

Whether you're looking for a quick bite or a gourmet meal, Portugal is sure to satisfy your cravings. With its fresh ingredients and flavorful dishes, the country is a culinary paradise.

SARAFINA PAWLAK

PORTUGAL TRAVEL GUIDE 2023

WHAT MAGICAL ABODE AWAITS ME IN PORTUGAL?

Portugal is a beautiful country that offers a wide array of accommodation options for travelers. Whether you are looking for a luxurious hotel, rustic cottage, or camping in the countryside, Portugal has something for everyone.

LUXURY HOTELS

Portugal boasts a number of stunning luxury hotels, many of which are located in popular holiday destinations such as the Algarve and Lisbon. These hotels typically offer a range of facilities including swimming pools, spa treatments, and fine dining restaurants. Many of these hotels also offer stunning views of beaches, mountains, or the cities. For a more exclusive experience, some luxury hotels offer private villas and suites, often with a private pool and garden.

BOUTIQUE HOTELS

If you're looking for something more unique, Portugal also has a range of boutique hotels. These smaller, independent hotels typically have fewer rooms than a traditional hotel and offer a more intimate atmosphere. Many of these hotels are located in rural areas, offering a chance to get away from the hustle and bustle of city life. Some of these boutique hotels offer exclusive spa treatments and fine dining options, while others may be more laid back, with rustic charm and local cuisine.

SARAFINA PAWLAK

PORTUGAL TRAVEL GUIDE 2023

HOSTELS

Portugal also has a range of hostels for budget-conscious travelers. These hostels often offer dormitory-style accommodation in shared rooms, as well as private rooms with en-suite bathrooms. Hostels are generally located in cities and towns, and usually have a lively atmosphere with plenty of activities and social events.

APARTMENTS AND VILLAS

Renting an apartment or villa is a great option for travelers who want to have their own space and the freedom to explore on their own. Apartments can be rented for short term or long term stays, and many offer fully equipped kitchens, living rooms, and bedrooms. Villas come in a variety of sizes and are a great option for larger groups or families.

Camping

For travelers who prefer the great outdoors, Portugal offers a range of camping options. There are campsites located throughout the country, ranging from basic facilities to those with swimming pools and other amenities. Many of these campsites are within easy reach of beaches, mountains, and other attractions.

Whatever type of accommodation you choose, Portugal is sure to have something to suit your needs. From luxury hotels to camping in the countryside, you're sure to find the perfect place to stay.

SARAFINA PAWLAK

PORTUGAL TRAVEL GUIDE 2023

CHAPTER 6

EXPERIENCE THE WONDER OF PORTUGAL'S TRANSPORTATION SYSTEM – EXPLORE THE POSSIBILITIES OF WHERE IT WILL TAKE YOU!

Portugal, located in the westernmost part of the Iberian Peninsula, is a stunning country filled with stunning landscapes and beautiful cities. The country is well-connected by an extensive transport network and makes it easy to get around, no matter where you're traveling. From airports and train stations to buses and ferries, Portugal boasts a wide array of transportation options to get you from one destination to the next.

AIRPORTS

Portugal is home to a number of international airports, including Lisbon Portela Airport, Faro Airport, and Porto Airport. These airports offer direct flights to many cities around the world and are the best way to get to Portugal from abroad. Once you've arrived, there are a number of transportation options to help you get around the country.

TRAINS

Portugal has an extensive railway network that can take you from one city to the next. The trains are comfortable, reliable, and often the fastest way to get from A to B. The high-speed Alfa Pendular train is a great option for long-distance journeys, while the Intercidades train is great for short trips.

SARAFINA PAWLAK

PORTUGAL TRAVEL GUIDE 2023

BUSES

Buses are the most popular and most affordable way to get around Portugal. There are a number of bus companies that offer routes throughout the country, making it easy to get from one city to the next. The buses are comfortable and the tickets are affordable, so it's a great option for budget travelers.

FERRIES

Ferries are a great way to explore Portugal's coastal cities and islands. From the Azores to Madeira, there are a number of ferry routes that can take you to some of the country's most beautiful destinations. The ferries are comfortable and the views are breathtaking, so it's a great way to travel.

CAR RENTAL

If you're looking for a more flexible way to explore the country, then car rental is the way to go. There are a number of car rental companies throughout Portugal, and the prices are usually quite reasonable. This is a great option if you want to explore the country at your own pace.

TAXI

Taxis are also a great way to get around Portugal. The fares are usually quite affordable and the drivers are often knowledgeable about the local area. This is a great option if you're looking for a more convenient way to get from one place to the next.

SARAFINA PAWLAK

PORTUGAL TRAVEL GUIDE 2023

No matter how you choose to get around Portugal, you're sure to have an unforgettable time. From airports and train stations to buses and ferries, the country is well-connected and makes it easy to get around. So, get out there and explore all that Portugal has to offer.

SARAFINA PAWLAK

CHAPTER 7

THE BEAUTY OF PORTUGAL'S OUTDOORS IS INCOMPARABLE

Portugal is an incredibly diverse country with a wide array of outdoor activities to offer. From the lush green valleys of the north to the sunny beaches of the south, there is something for everyone. Whether you're a nature lover, an adventurous thrill-seeker or just someone looking for a relaxing day in the sun, Portugal has plenty of outdoor activities to keep you entertained.

For nature lovers, Portugal is home to some of the most beautiful national parks in

Europe. The Peneda-Gerês National Park is the largest in Portugal, situated in the far north of the country and boasting stunning landscapes, rich wildlife and ancient villages. The Serra da Estrela Natural Park is another great choice, offering breathtaking views of the Portuguese mountains and a variety of activities such as hiking, cycling, rock climbing and skiing.

If you're an adventurous traveler, there are plenty of activities to keep you busy. Portugal has some of the best surfing in Europe and the Algarve region is home to some of the best waves in the world. For those looking for a bit more of a thrill, you can also go kayaking, paragliding, and even try your hand at some of the world's best big-wave surfing.

SARAFINA PAWLAK

PORTUGAL TRAVEL GUIDE 2023

For those looking for a more relaxing day outdoors, there are plenty of options. Portugal's golden beaches are perfect for soaking up the sun and enjoying a refreshing swim in the Atlantic Ocean. You can also explore the beautiful Portuguese countryside, take a boat trip along the Tagus River, or visit some of the country's many wineries.

No matter what type of outdoor activity you're looking for, Portugal has something for everyone. From the stunning landscapes of the national parks to the adrenaline-fueled thrills of surfing and paragliding, this country has something for everyone to enjoy

HISTORICAL SITES

Portugal is a country with a rich history and culture, and it is home to some of the most fascinating historical sites in Europe. From prehistoric megalithic monuments to medieval castles, these sites offer visitors a glimpse into the country's past. Here is a guide to some of the best historical sites to visit in Portugal.

SINTRA

Sintra is a small town located about 30 kilometers from Lisbon. It is home to some of the most amazing historical sites in Portugal. The most famous is the Palácio Nacional de Sintra, a castle built in the 15th century by the Portuguese royal family.

SARAFINA PAWLAK

Other interesting sites include the Convento dos Capuchos, a monastery built in the 16th century; the National Palace of Queluz, a former royal residence; and the Castelo dos Mouros, a Moorish castle that was built in the 8th century.

LISBON

Lisbon is Portugal's capital and one of the oldest cities in Europe. It is home to many historical sites, including the Jerónimos Monastery, a 16th-century monastery built in the Manueline style; the Castelo de São Jorge, a Moorish castle dating back to the 11th century; and the Torre de Belém, a 16th-century lighthouse. There are also several museums in Lisbon, such as the National Museum of Ancient Art, the

National Tile Museum, and the National
Coach Museum.

SARAFINA PAWLAK

PORTUGAL TRAVEL GUIDE 2023

CHAPTER 8

DISCOVER PORTUGAL'S HISTORIC GEMS

PORTO

Located in northern Portugal, Porto is a port city with a long history. The historical center of Porto is a UNESCO World Heritage Site and is home to many important historical sites, such as the São Bento Train Station, the Ribeira District, and the Palácio da Bolsa. Other interesting sites include the São Francisco Church, a Baroque-style church built in the 18th century, and the Torre dos Clérigos, a bell tower built in the 18th century.

EVORA

Evora is a small city in the Alentejo region of Portugal. It is home to some of the country's most spectacular historical sites, such as the Roman Temple of Évora, a temple built in the 1st century AD; the Aqueduto de Évora, an aqueduct built in the 16th century; the Cathedral of Évora, a Gothic cathedral built in the 13th century; and the Chapel of Bones, a chapel decorated with human bones.

COIMBRA

Coimbra is a city in central Portugal that is home to the country's oldest university, the University of Coimbra. The city is full of historical sites, such as the Old Cathedral, a Romanesque cathedral built in the 12th century; the Monastery of Santa Cruz, a monastery built in the 12th century; and

SARAFINA PAWLAK

PORTUGAL TRAVEL GUIDE 2023

the Church of Santa Cruz, a Baroque church built in the 17th century.

These are just a few of the many historical sites in Portugal. Whether you're looking for ancient monuments, medieval castles, or Baroque churches, you'll find them in this beautiful country. So if you're planning a trip to Portugal, be sure to visit some of these amazing historical sites.

COMMUNICATION

Communication is an integral part of any travel experience, and Portugal is no exception. As a country whos e culture has been shaped by centuries of cultural exchange and immigration, Portugal has a diverse language landscape that reflects its rich history.

The official language of Portugal is Portuguese, a Romance language that is the sixth most spoken native language in the world. It is spoken by the majority of the population and is the language used in most public and private institutions, as well as in the media.

SARAFINA PAWLAK

PORTUGAL TRAVEL GUIDE 2023

For travelers to Portugal, it is recommended that they learn at least some basic Portuguese phrases, as this will help them to communicate better with locals. Even if visitors do not speak Portuguese, they can usually find someone who speaks English, as this language is widely spoken throughout the country.

Despite Portuguese being the main language, there are a number of other languages spoken in Portugal, including Spanish, French, and German. These languages are especially common in tourist areas and in the major cities, where many people are bilingual.

In addition to language, there are a number of other communication strategies that visitors should be aware of when traveling to Portugal. For example, Portuguese people tend to communicate in a more informal and direct manner, so visitors should be aware of the need to be polite and respectful when speaking with locals.

Overall, communication in Portugal is an important part of any travel experience. Whether visitors are trying to learn Portuguese, or need help navigating their way around the country, they can rest assured that they will be able to communicate effectively with locals.

SARAFINA PAWLAK

PORTUGAL TRAVEL GUIDE 2023

CHAPTER 9

CONCLUSION

In conclusion, Portugal is a country that is full of life, culture, and beauty. It offers a unique and unforgettable experience with its exquisite architecture, stunning landscapes, rich history, and vibrant nightlife.

Whether you wish to explore the historical sites in Lisbon, relax on the beaches of the Algarve, or explore the vineyards in the Douro Valley, Portugal is the perfect destination for any traveler. There is something for everyone due to its varied selection of activities.

From the gastronomic delights to the breathtaking views, Portugal is a country that will leave you with memories that will last a lifetime. So, if you are looking for an adventure, a holiday destination, or simply a break from the mundane, travel to Portugal and explore the wonders it has to offer.

SARAFINA PAWLAK

PORTUGAL TRAVEL GUIDE
2023

Printed in Great Britain
by Amazon

20929152R00051